One Thought a Day

Copyright ©

All rights reserved for **Paradise Publisher**.
No parts of this publication may be reproduced, distributed, or transmitted in any form, or by any means, including photocopying, recording or other electronic or mechanical methods, without prior written permission from the publisher.

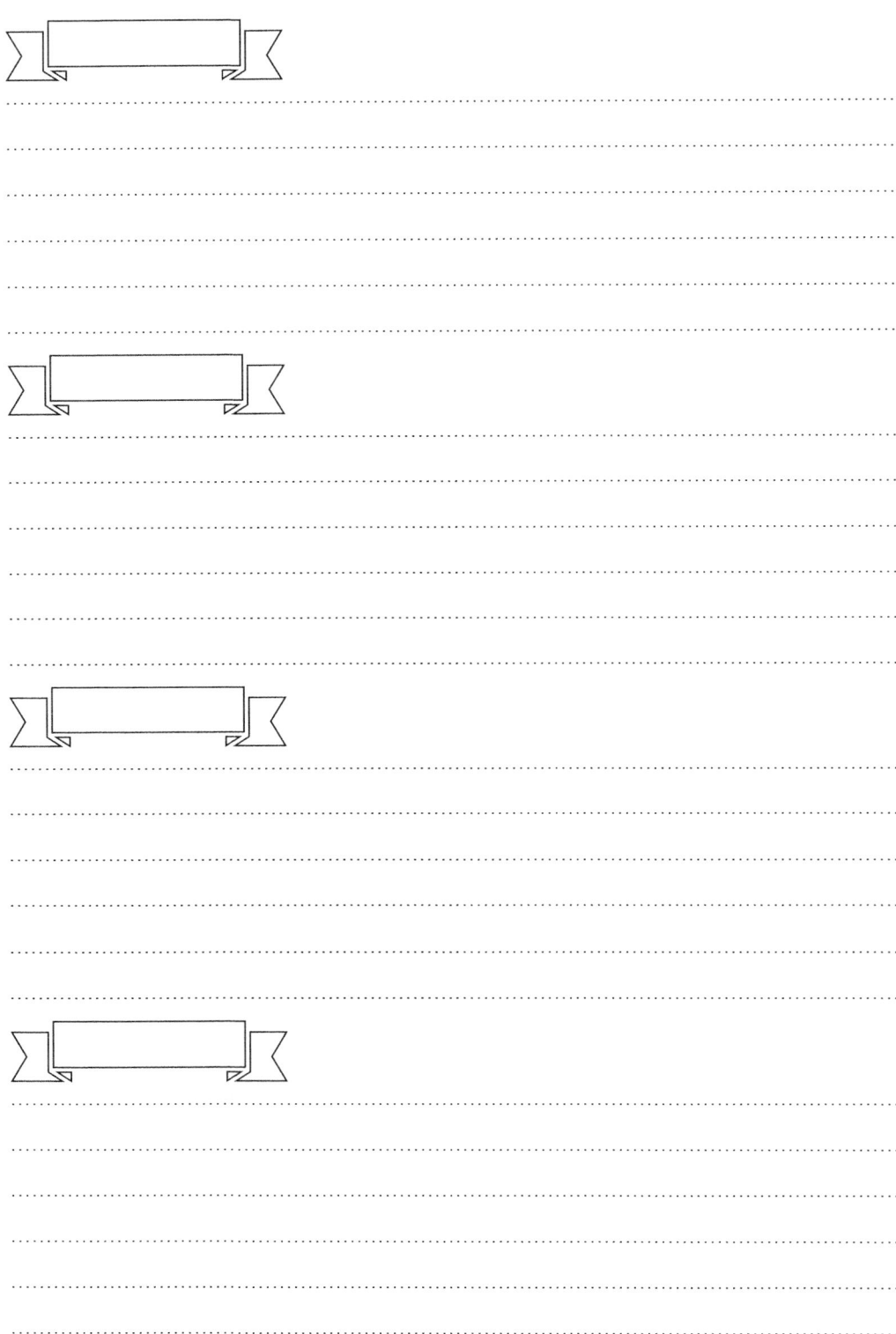

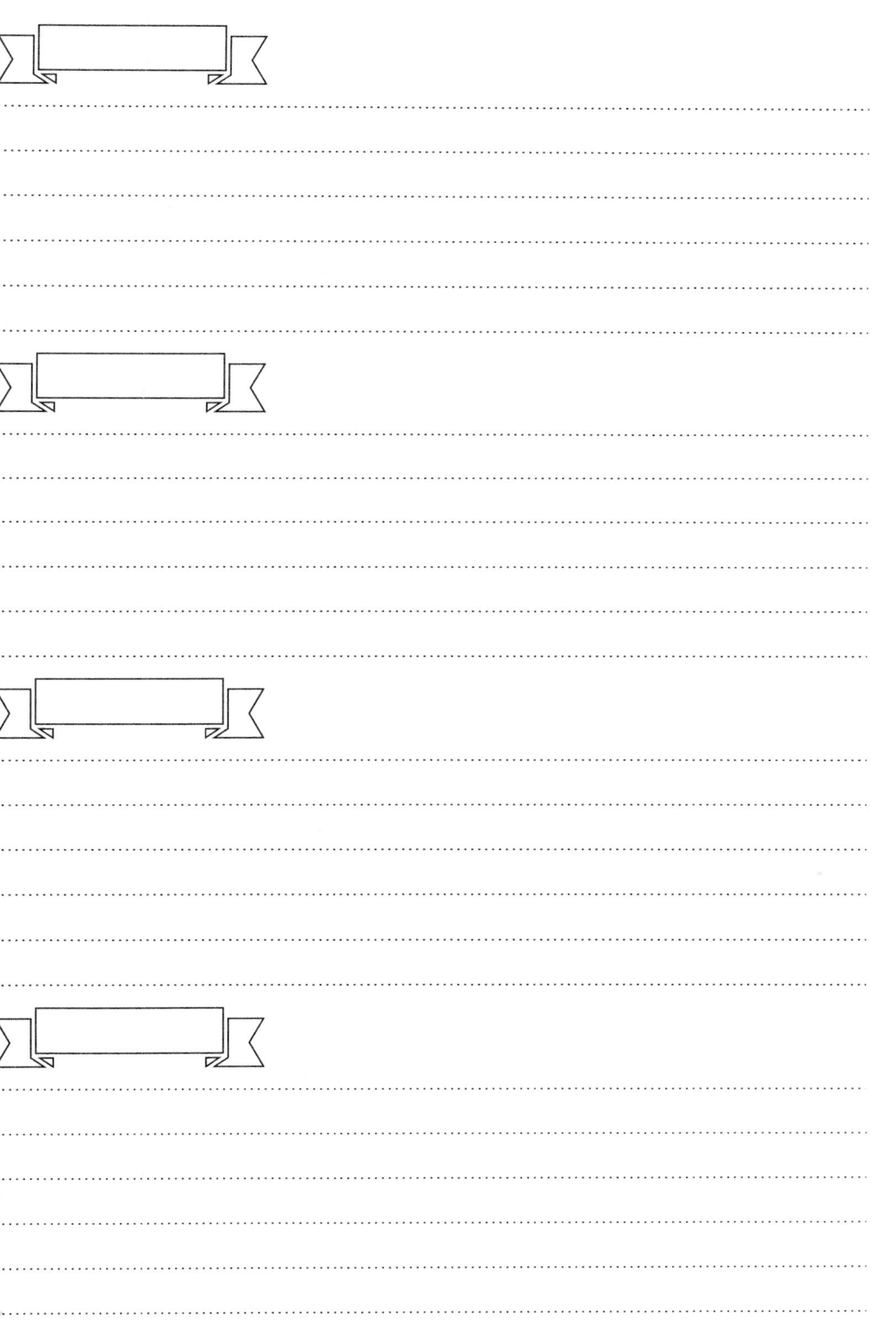

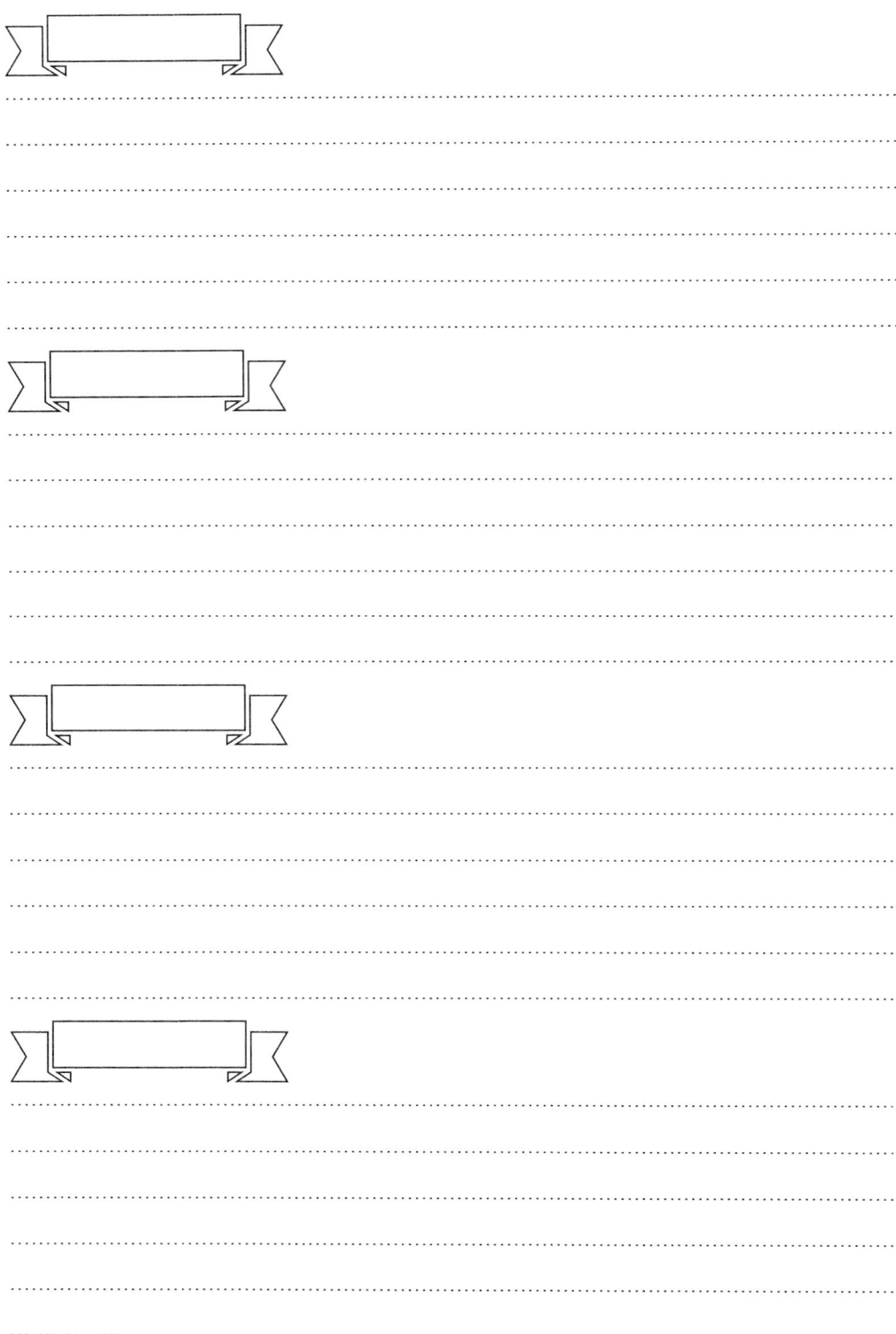

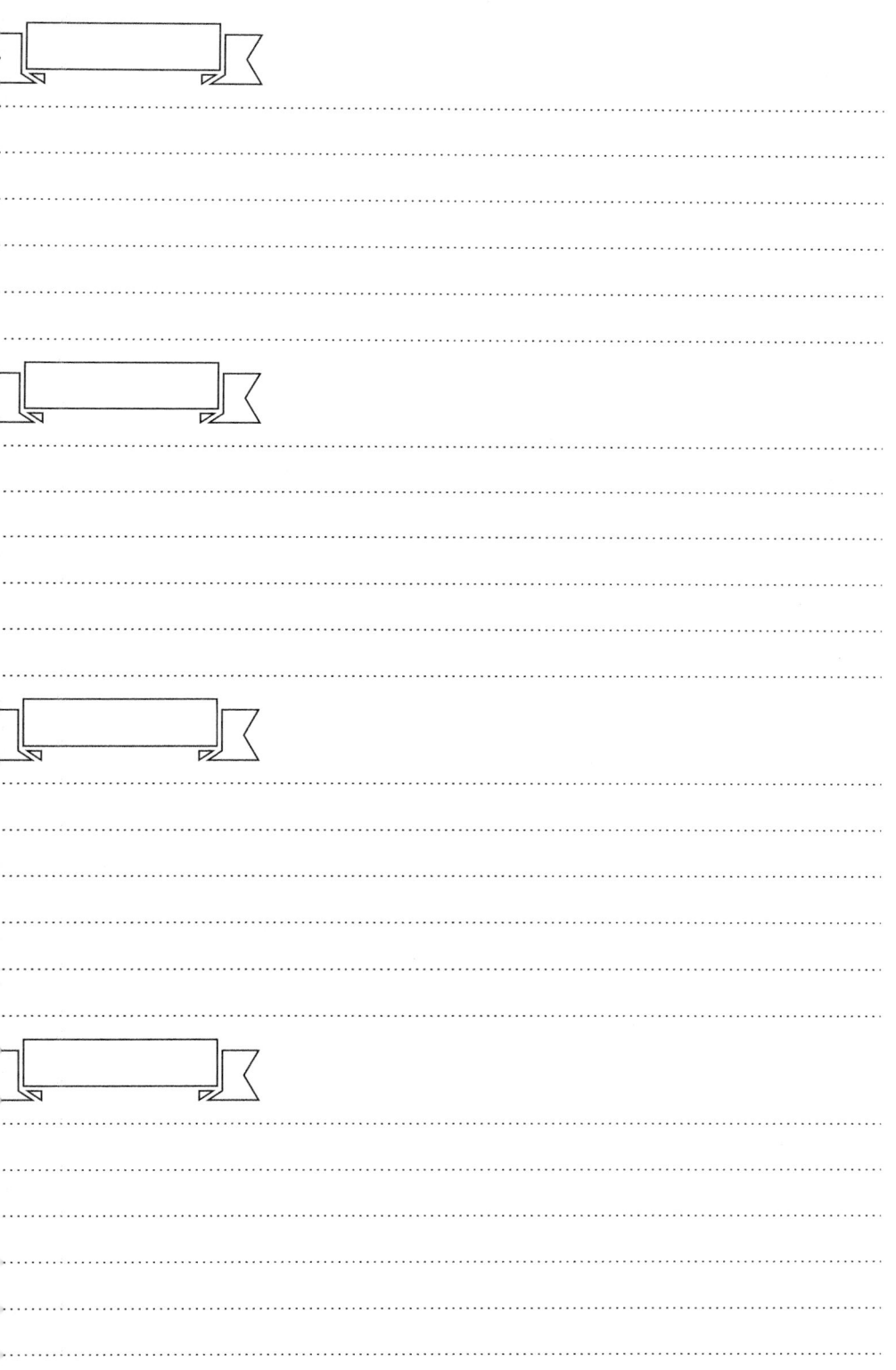

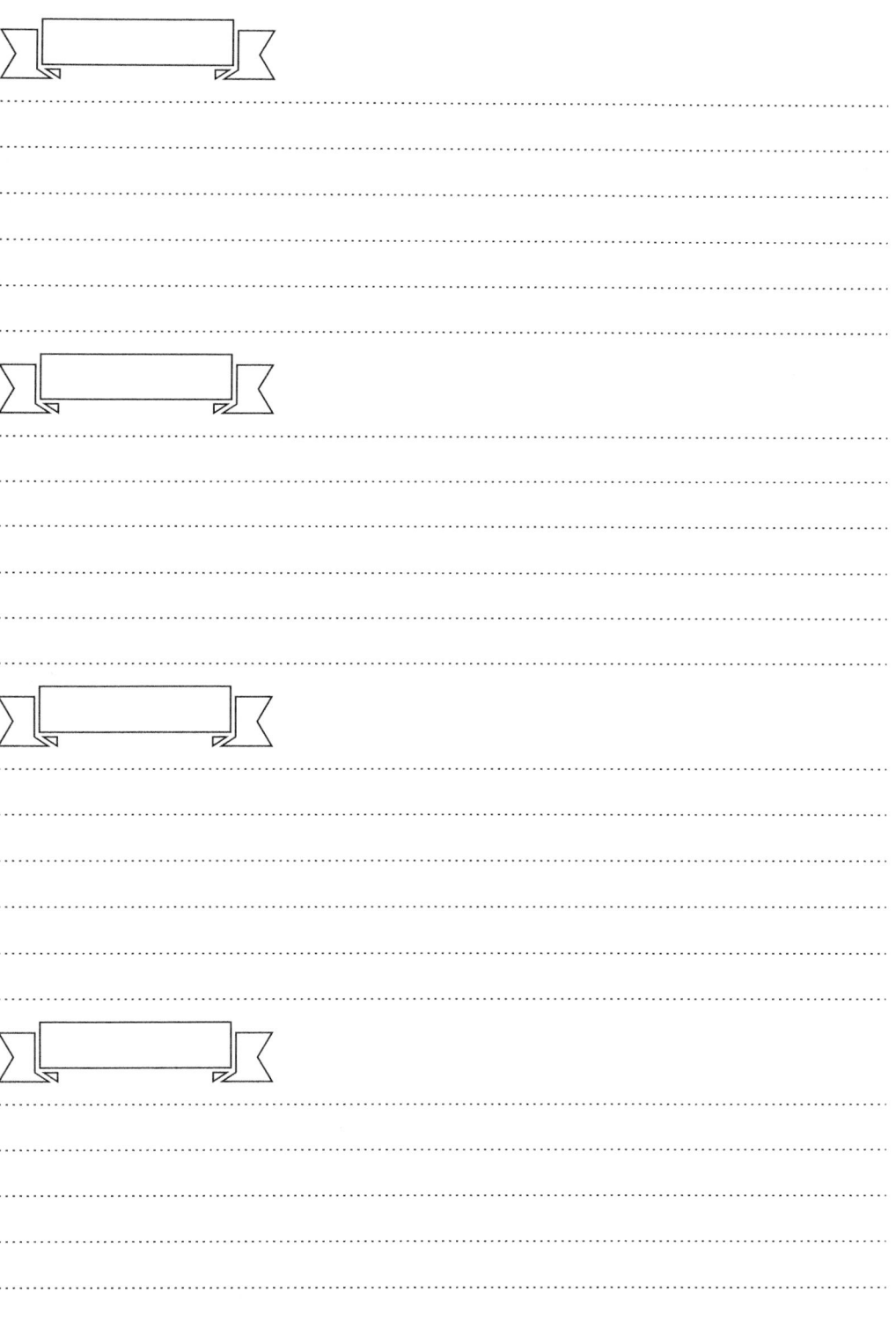

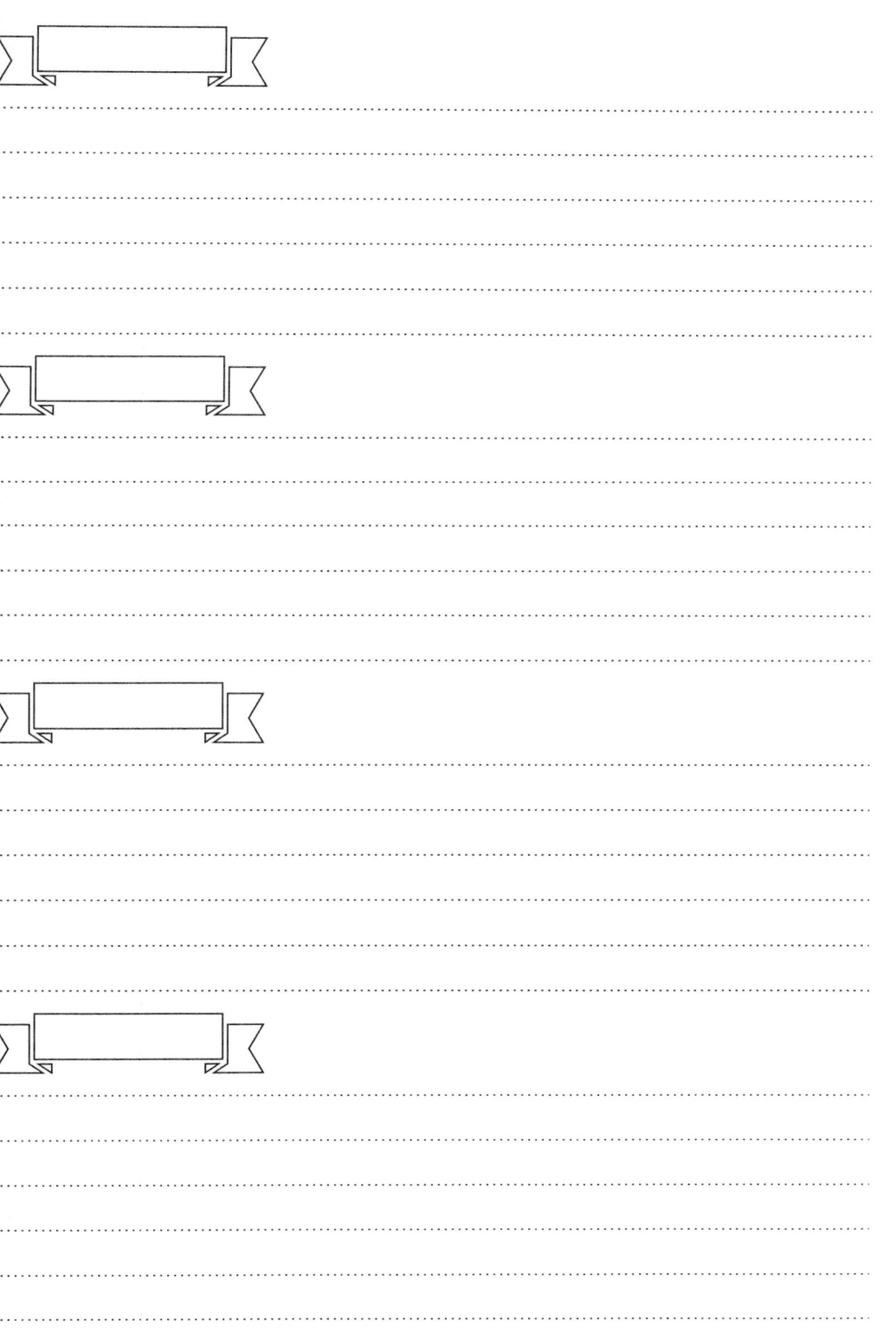

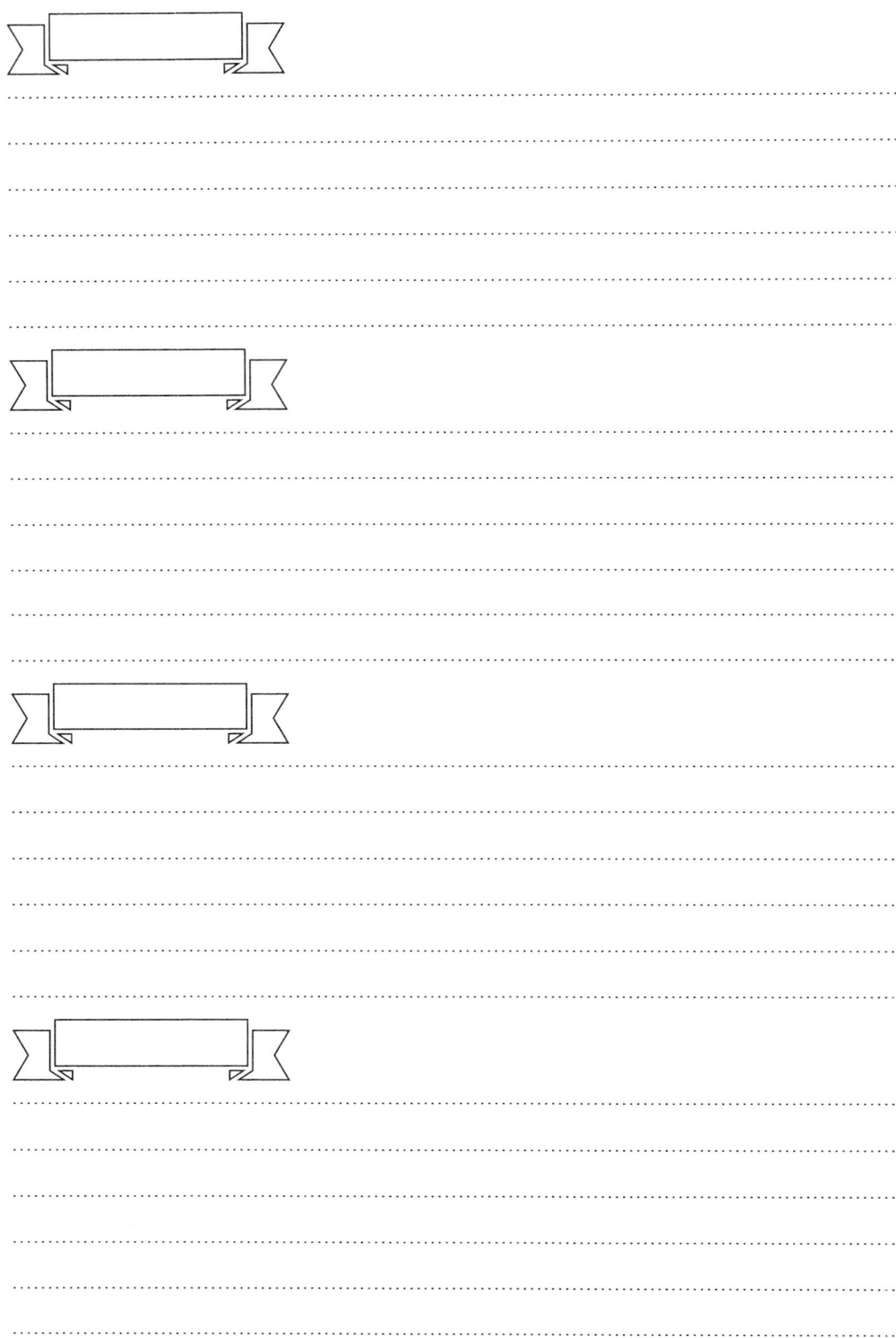

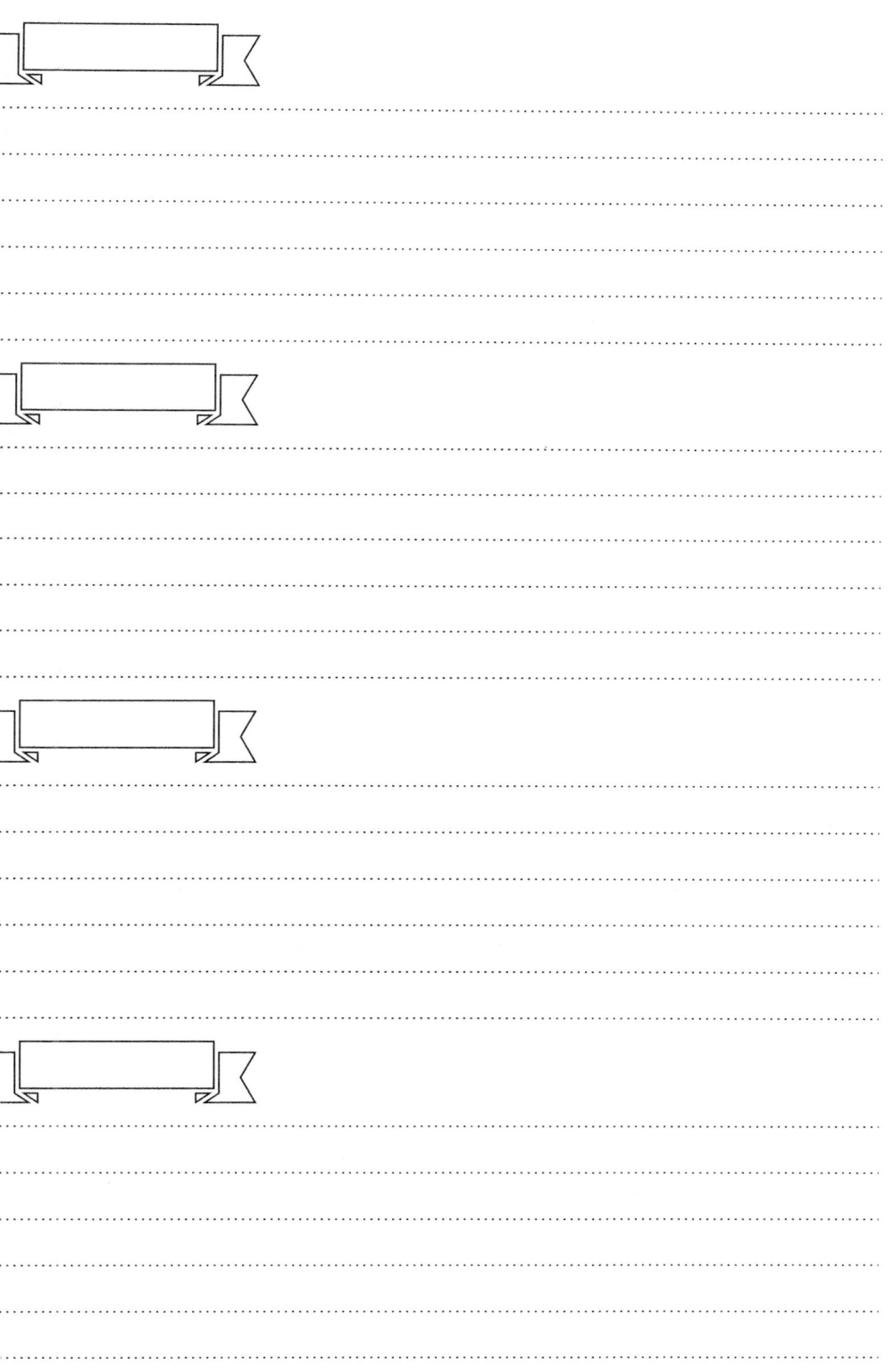

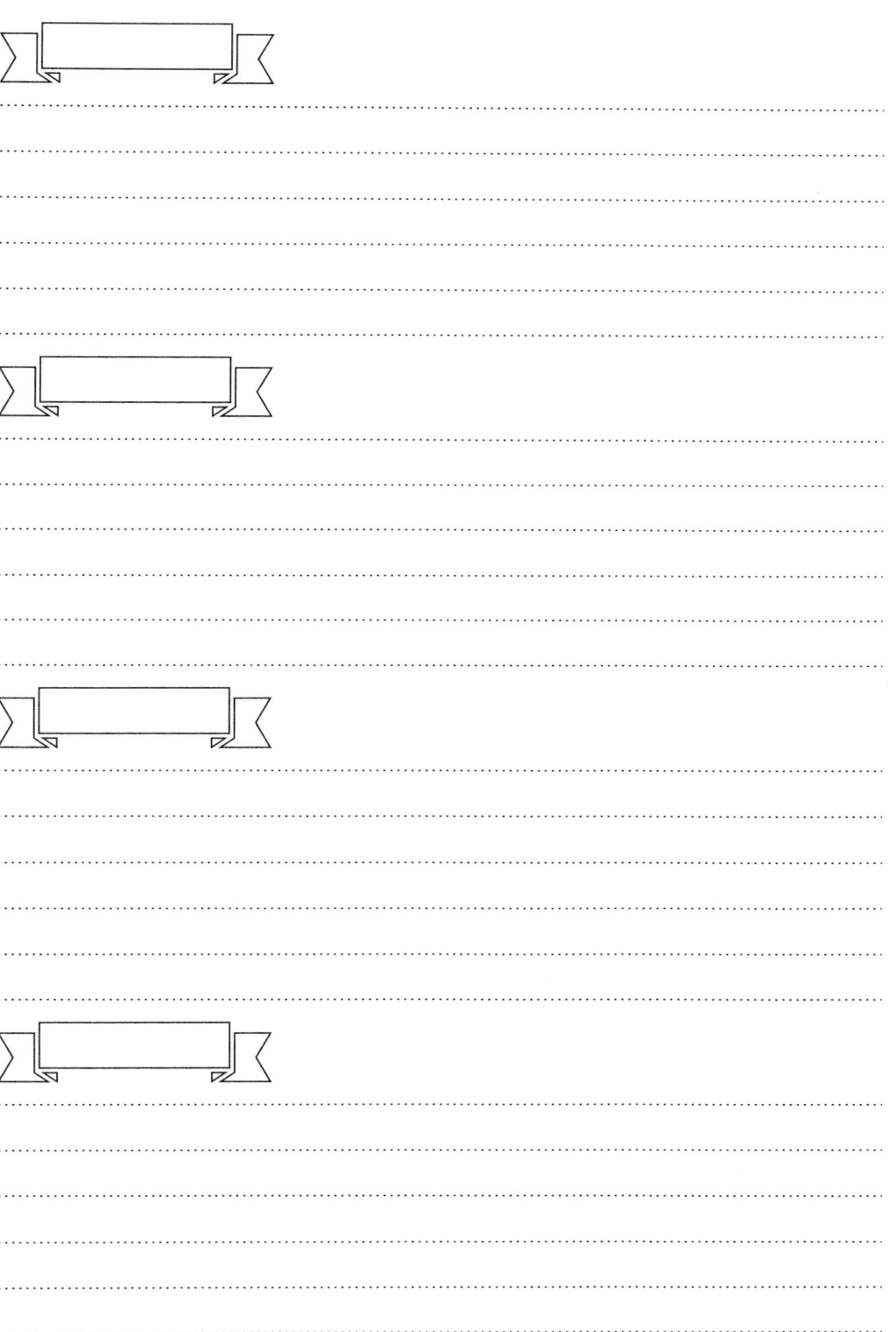

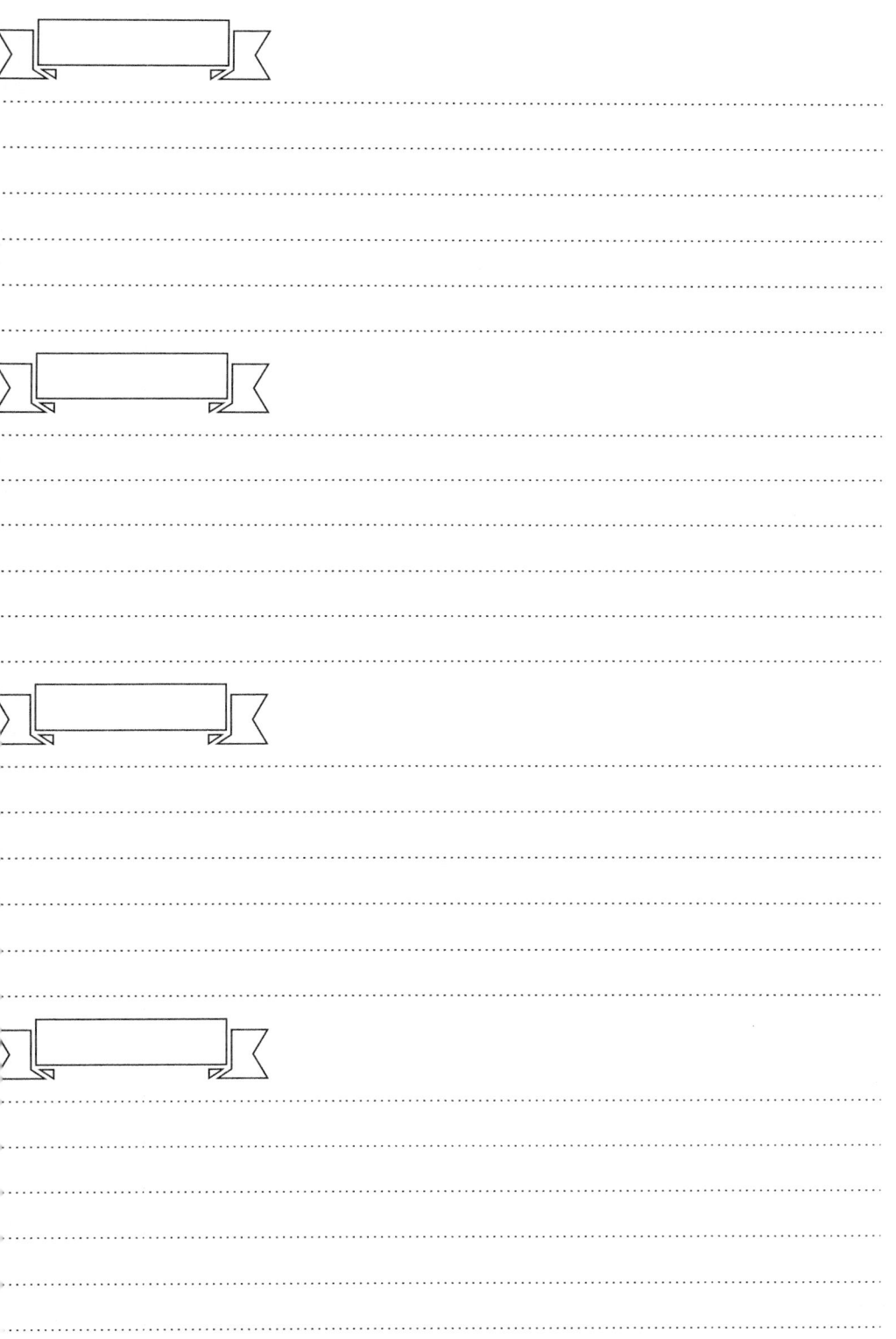

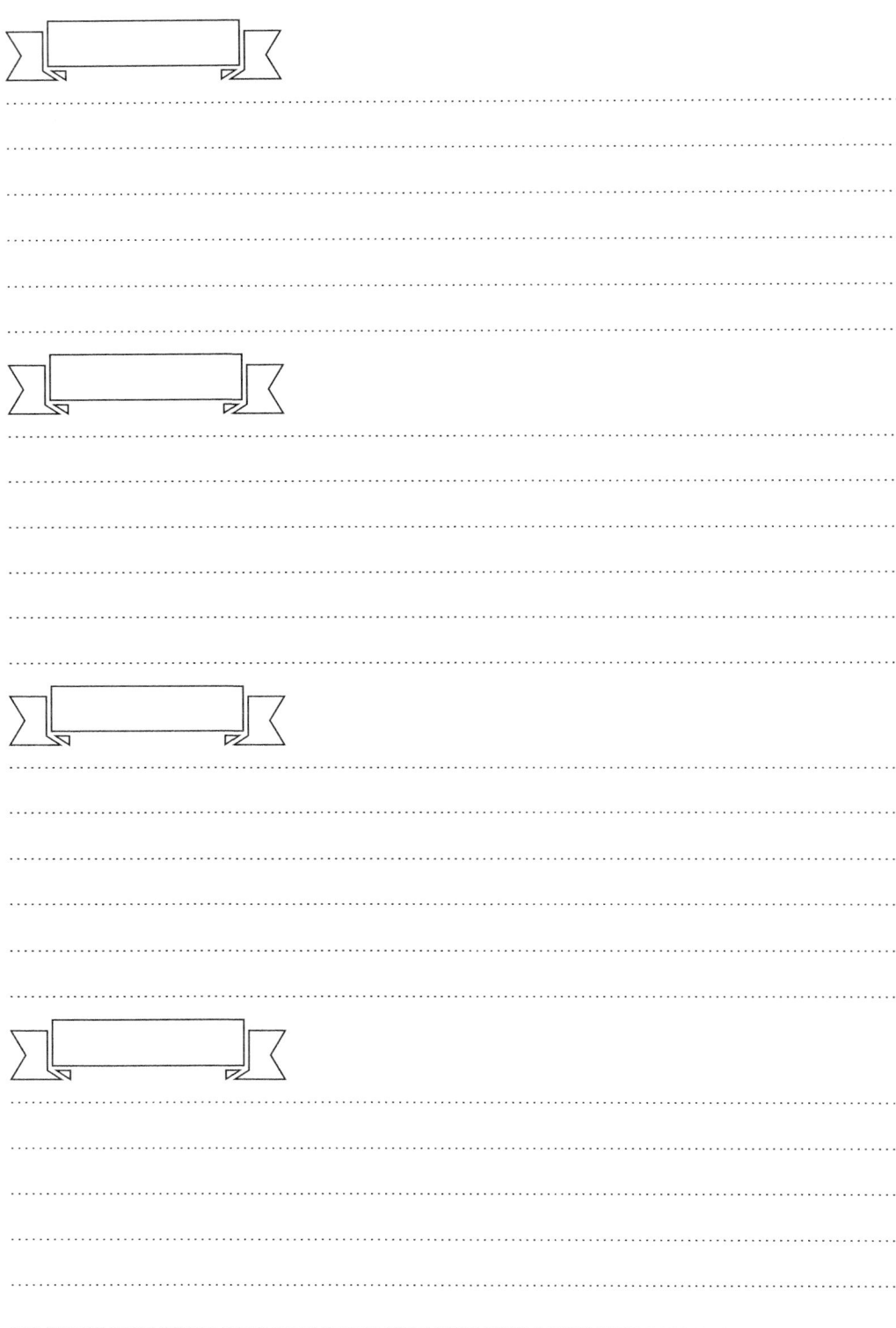

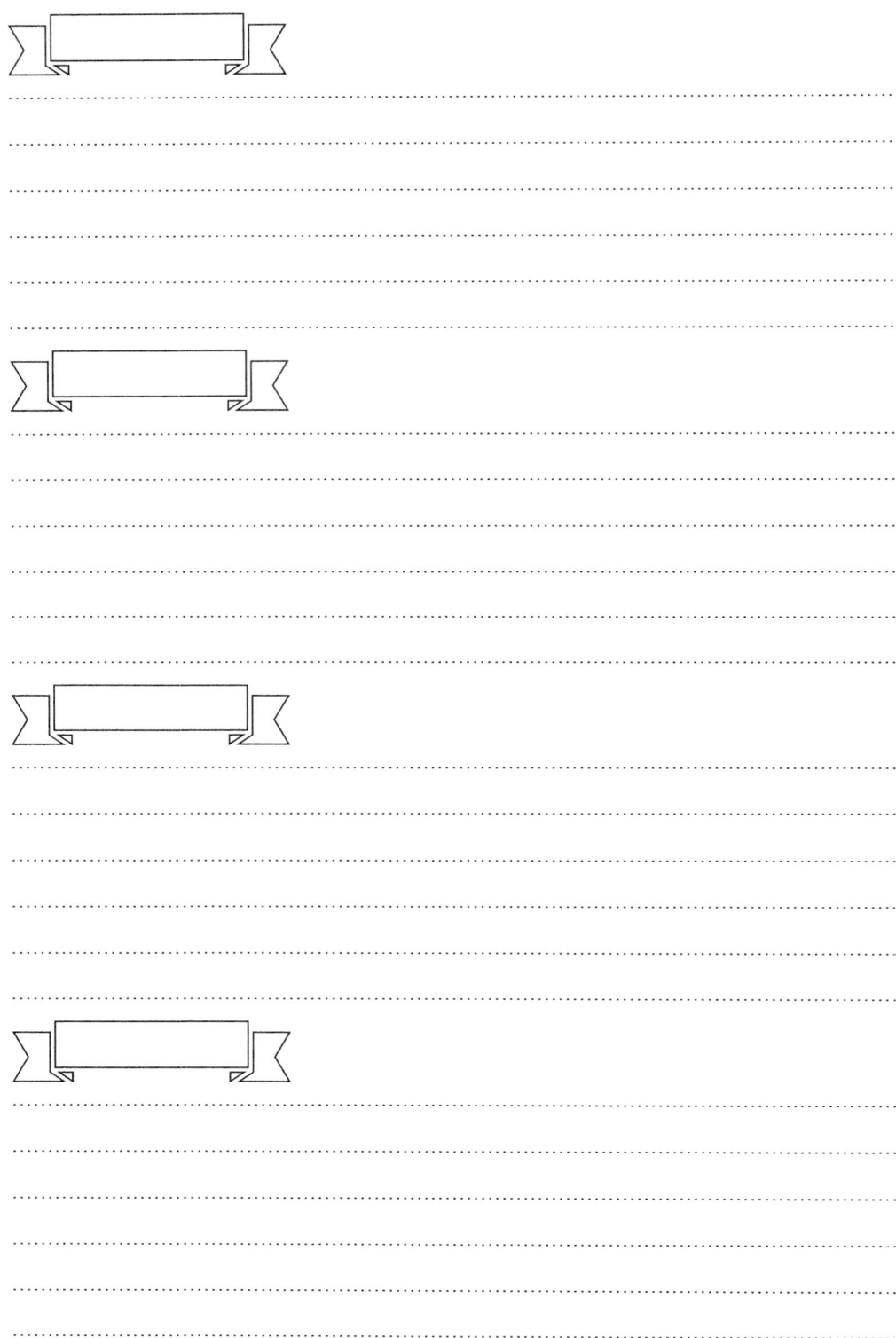

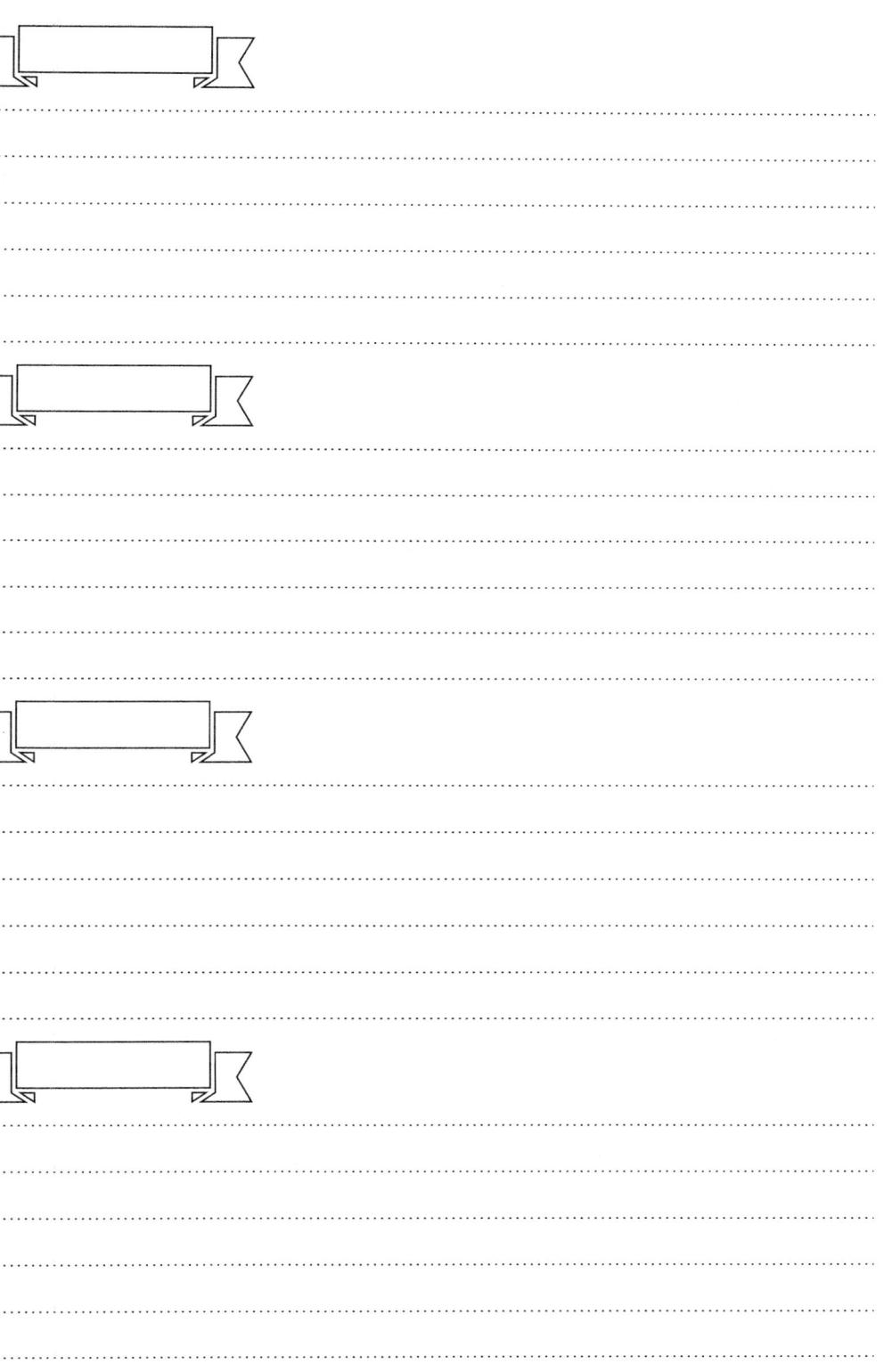

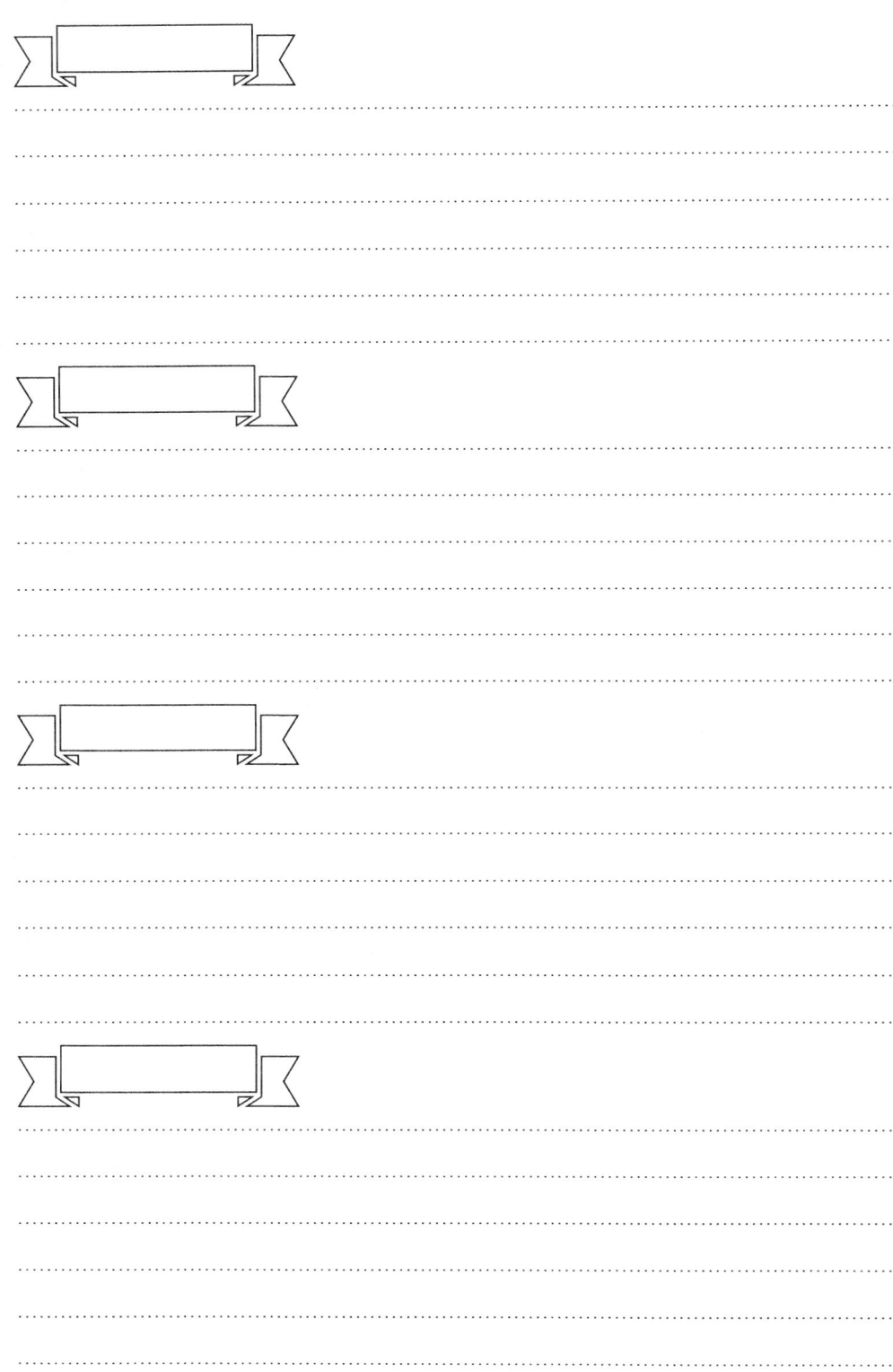

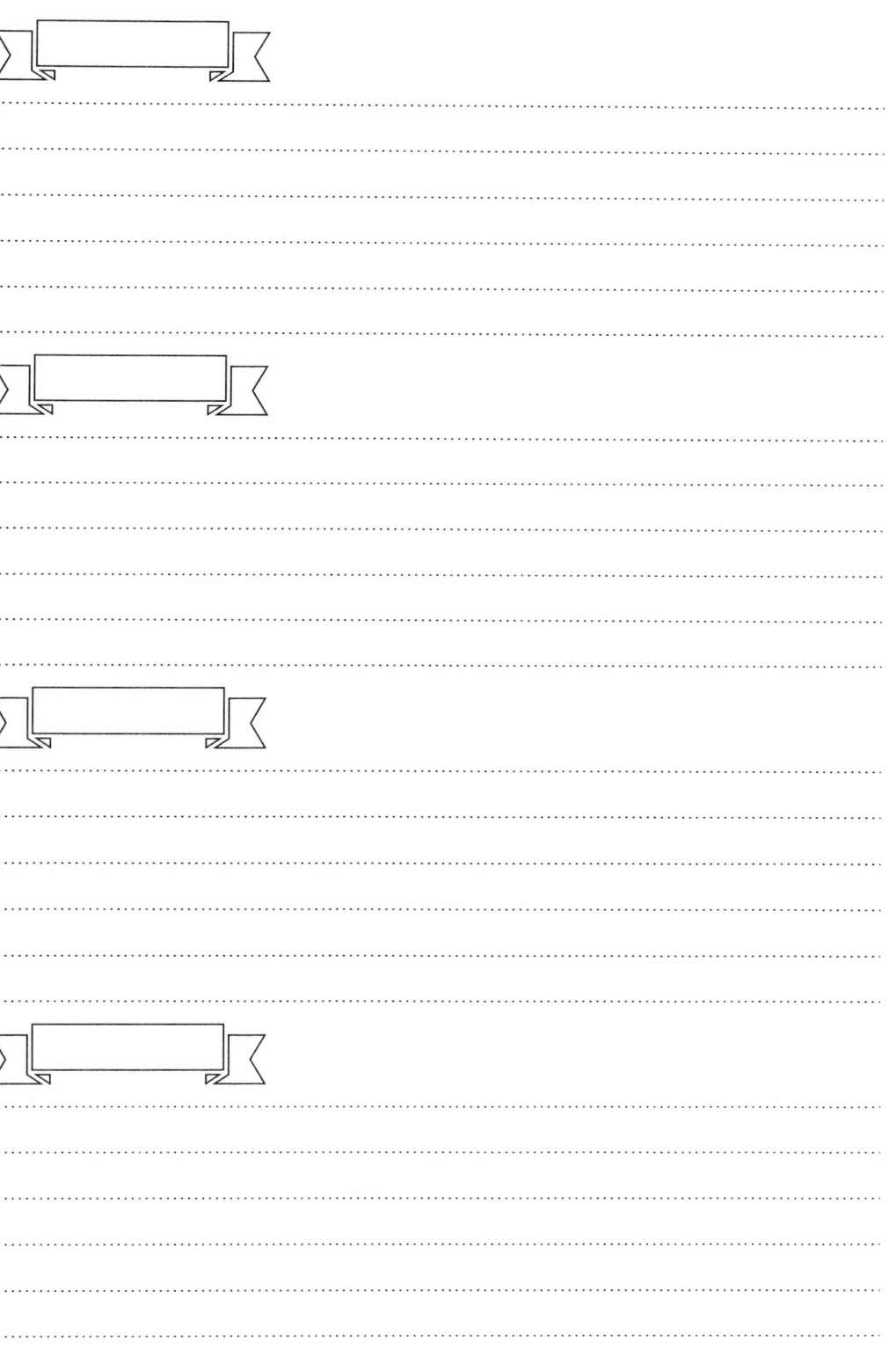

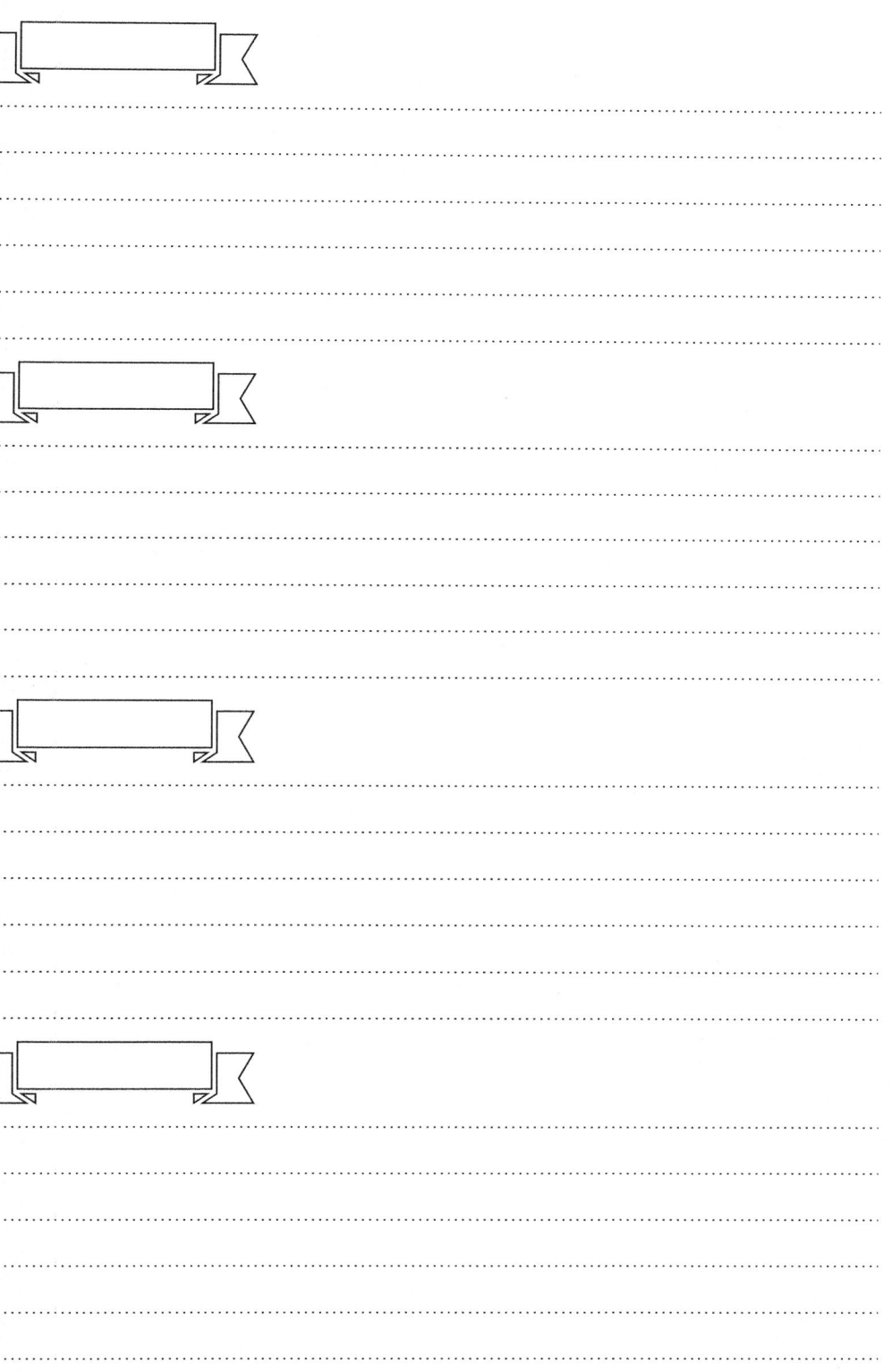

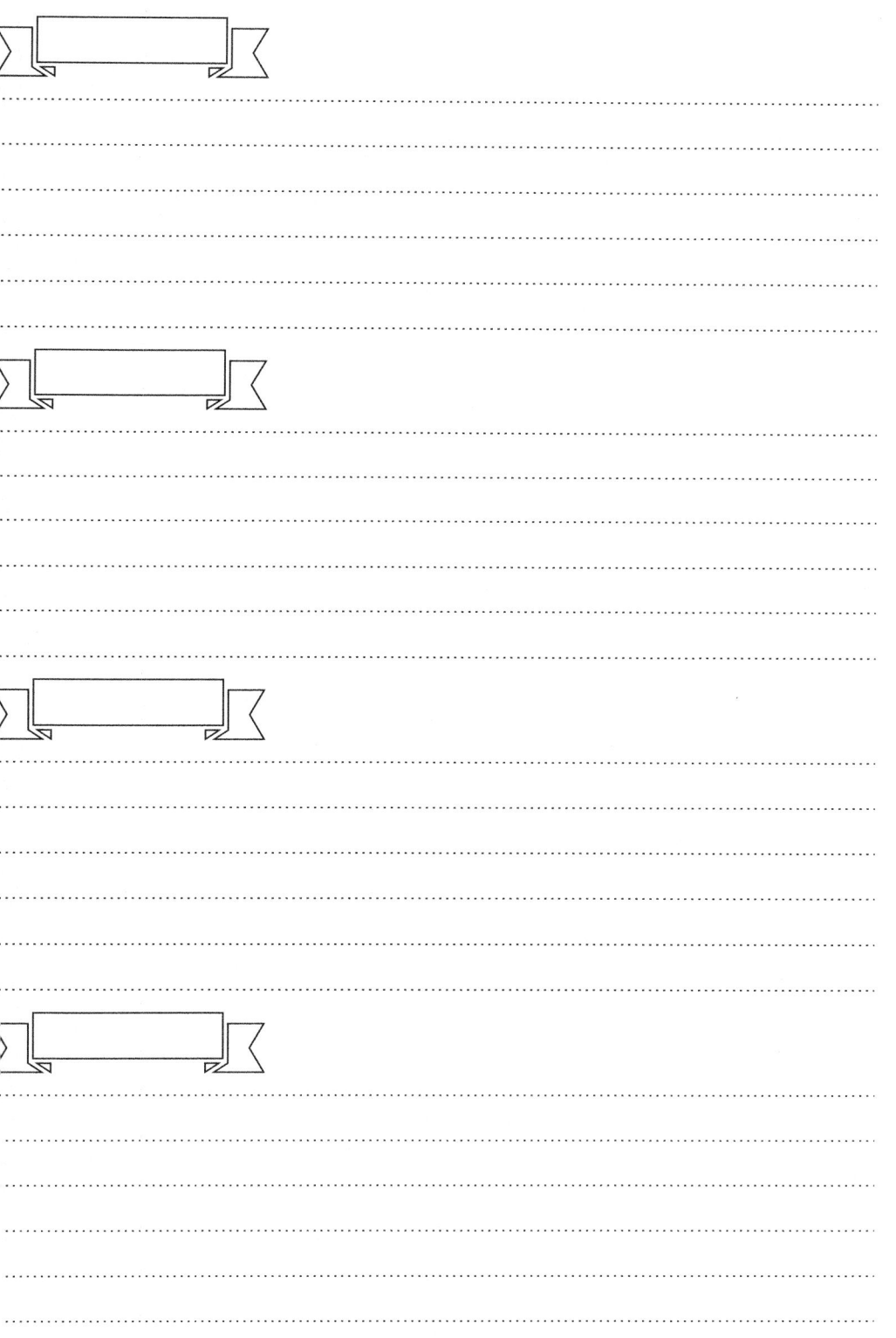

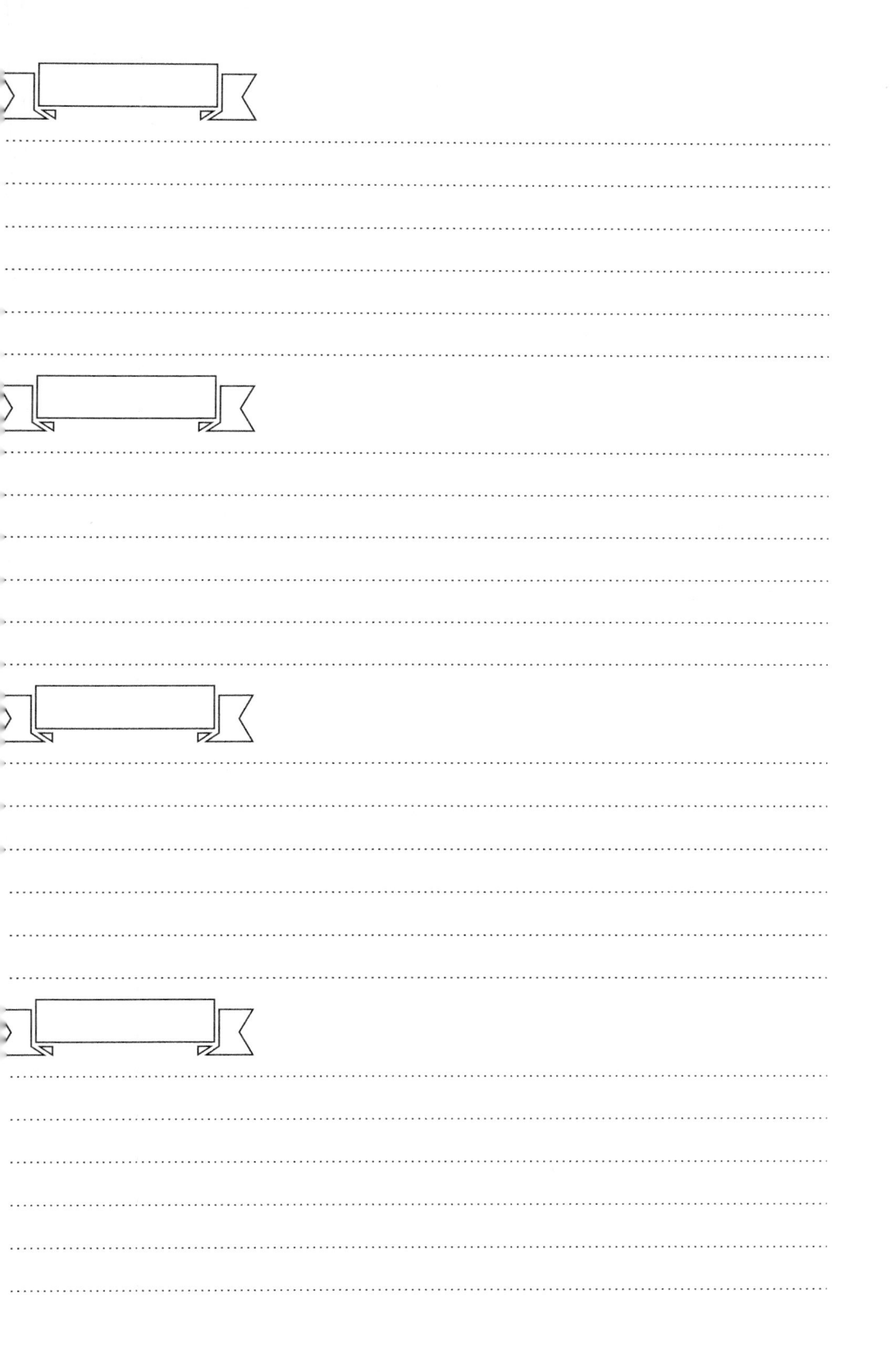

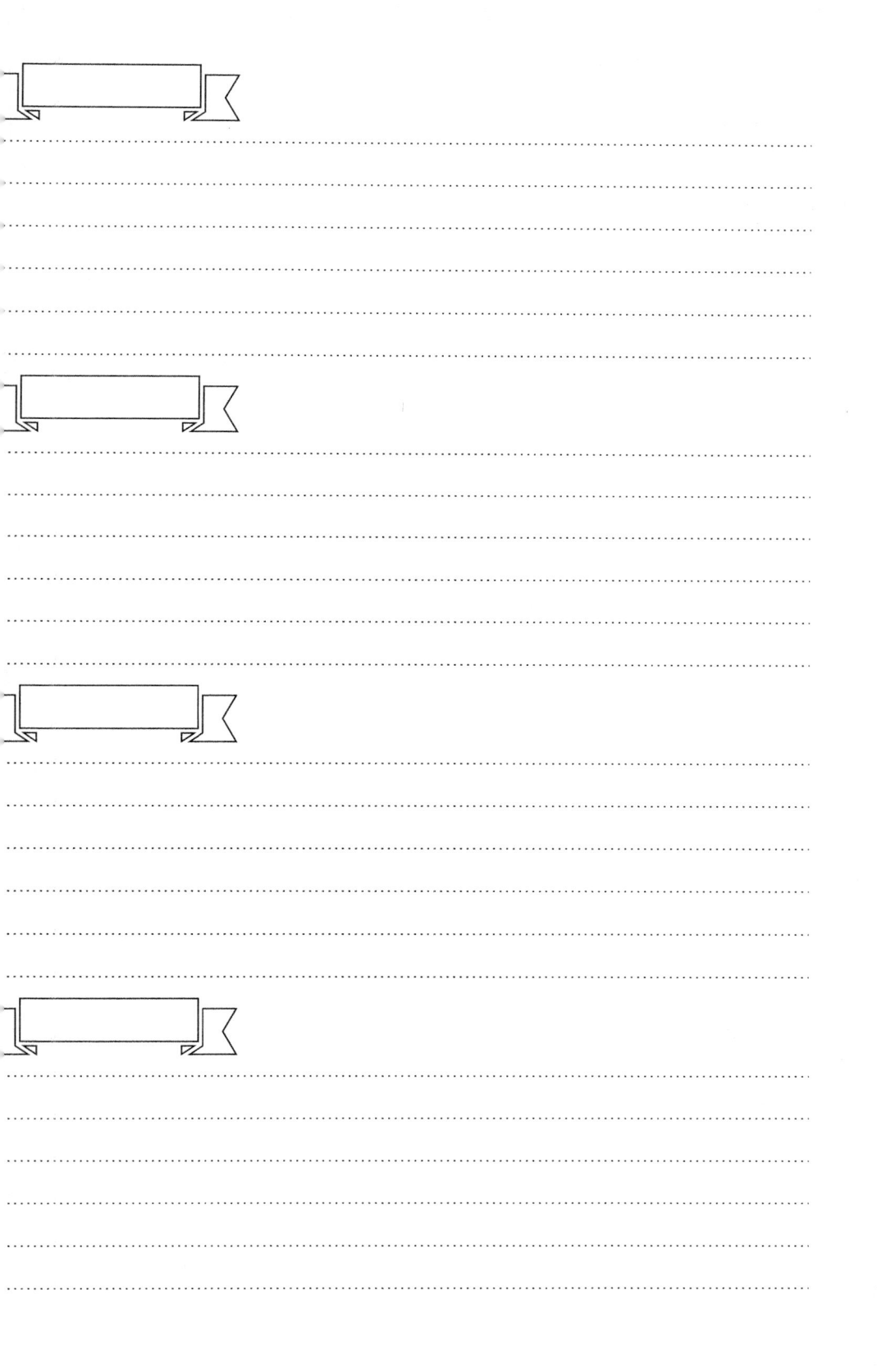

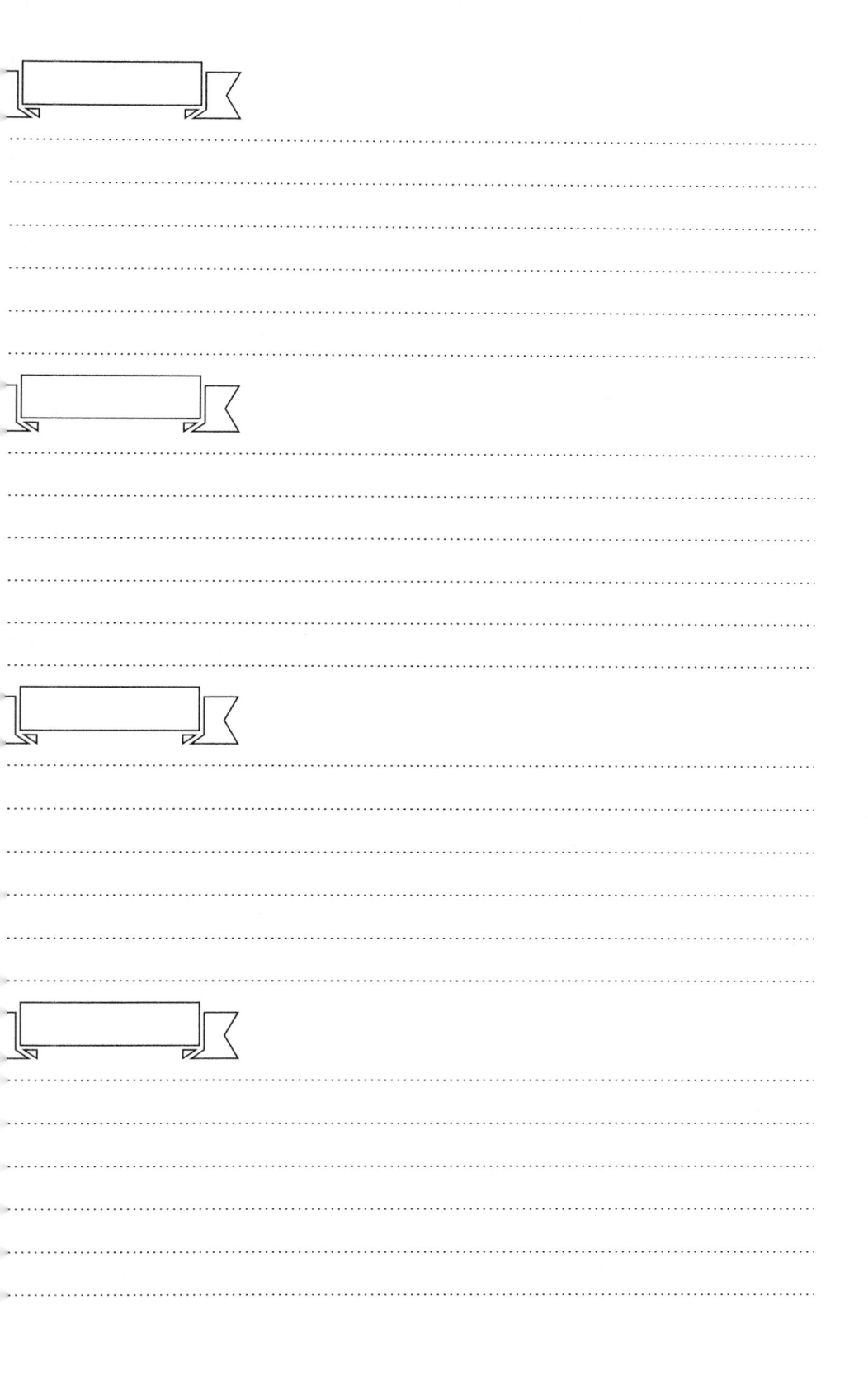

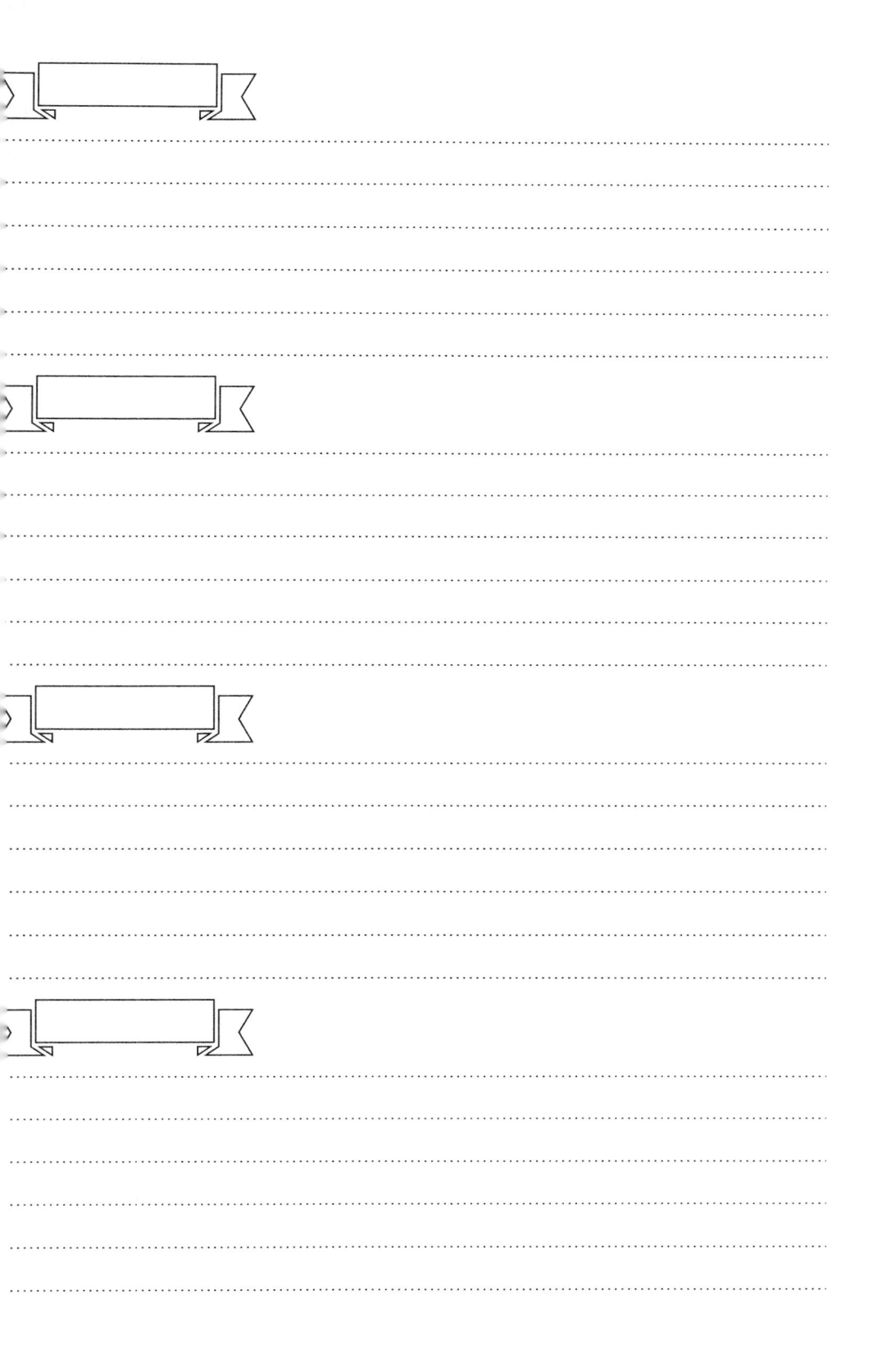

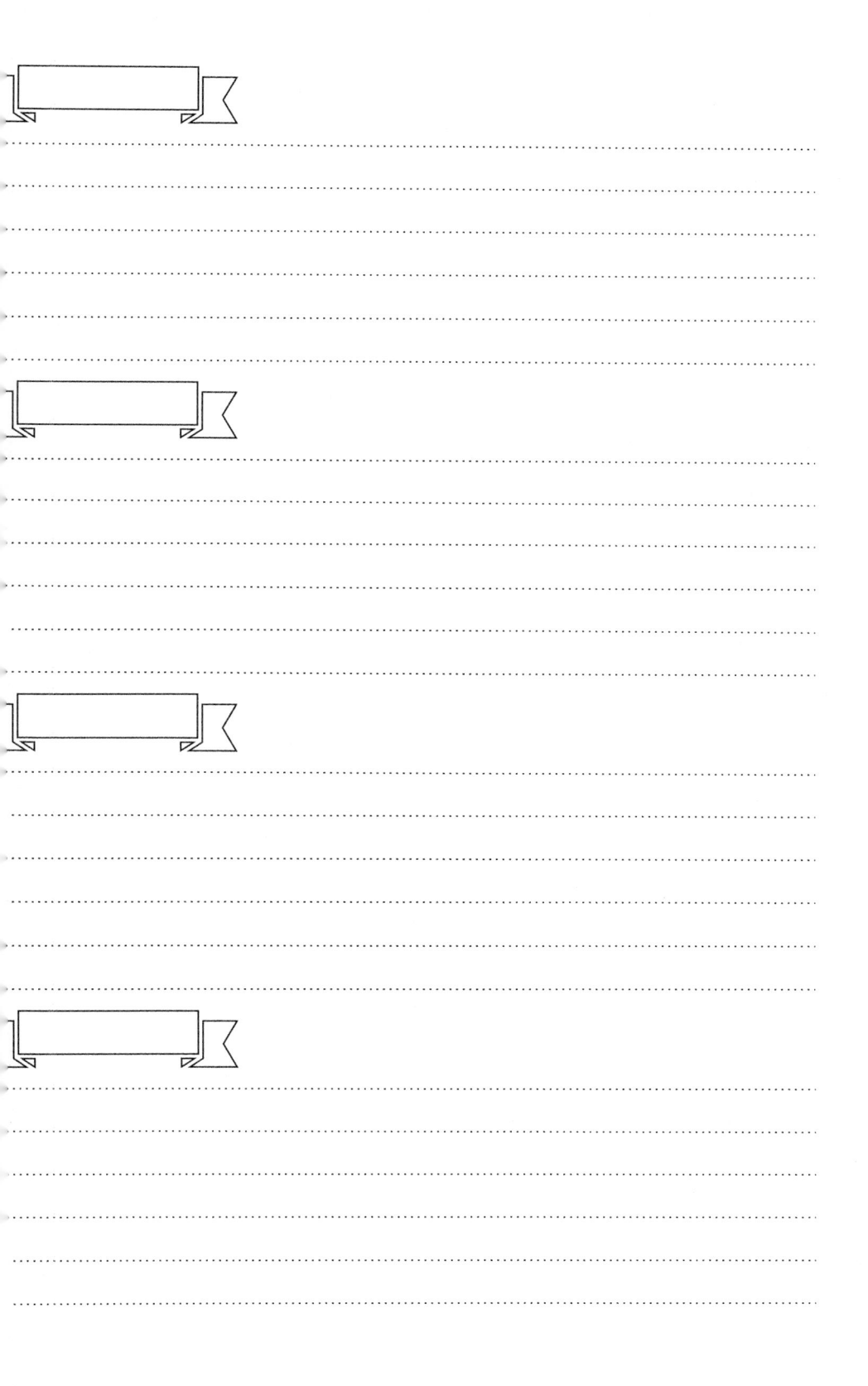

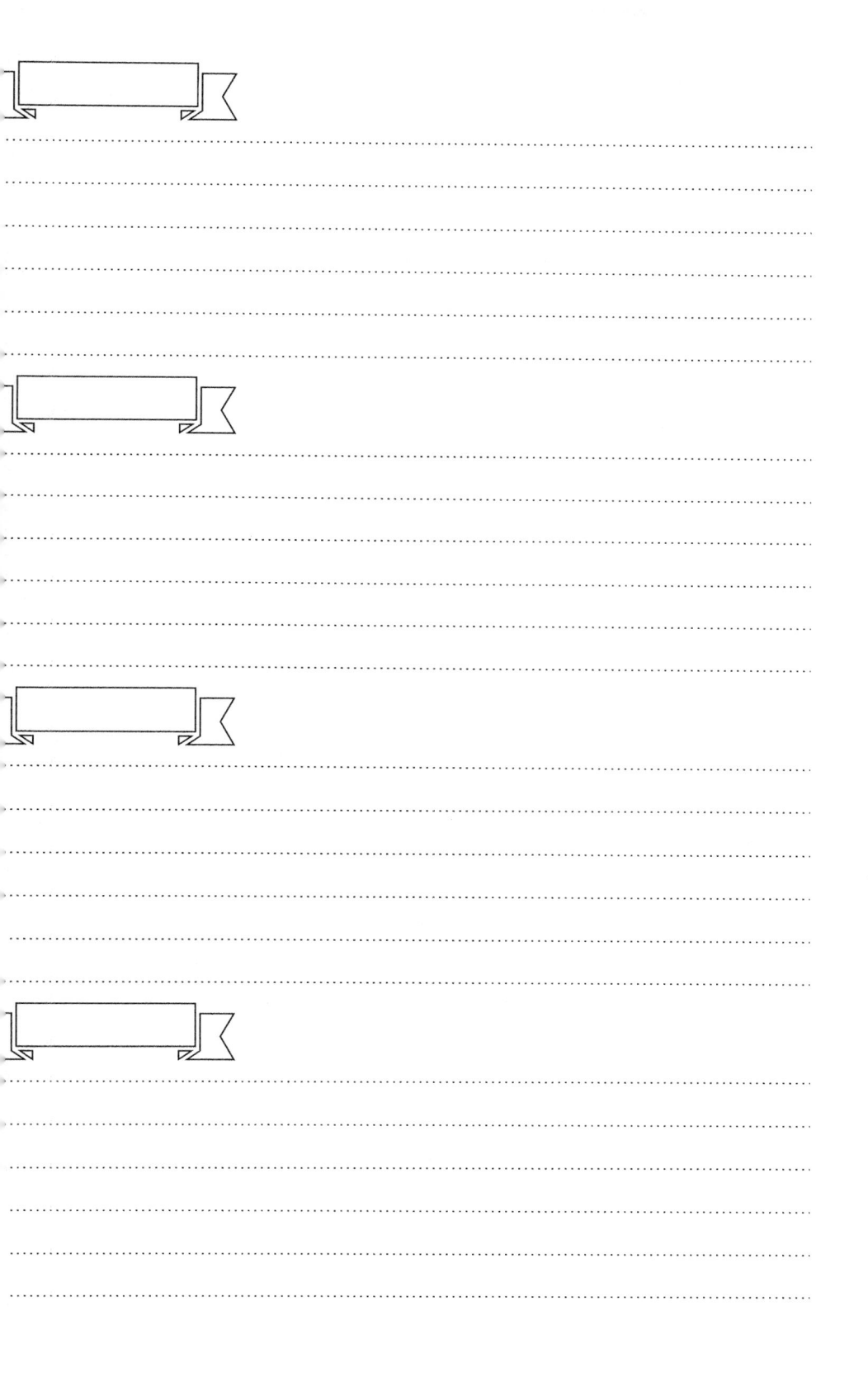

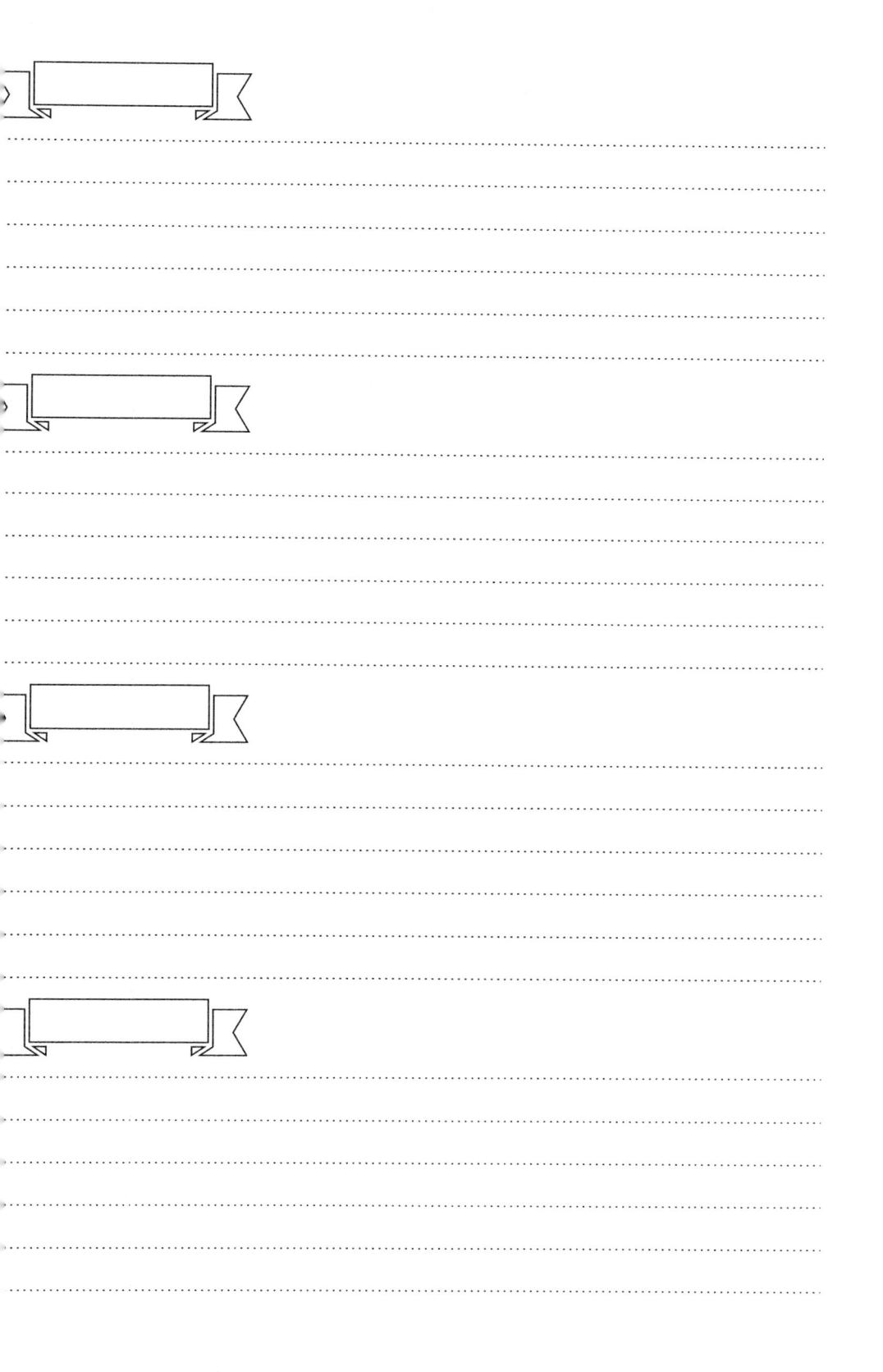

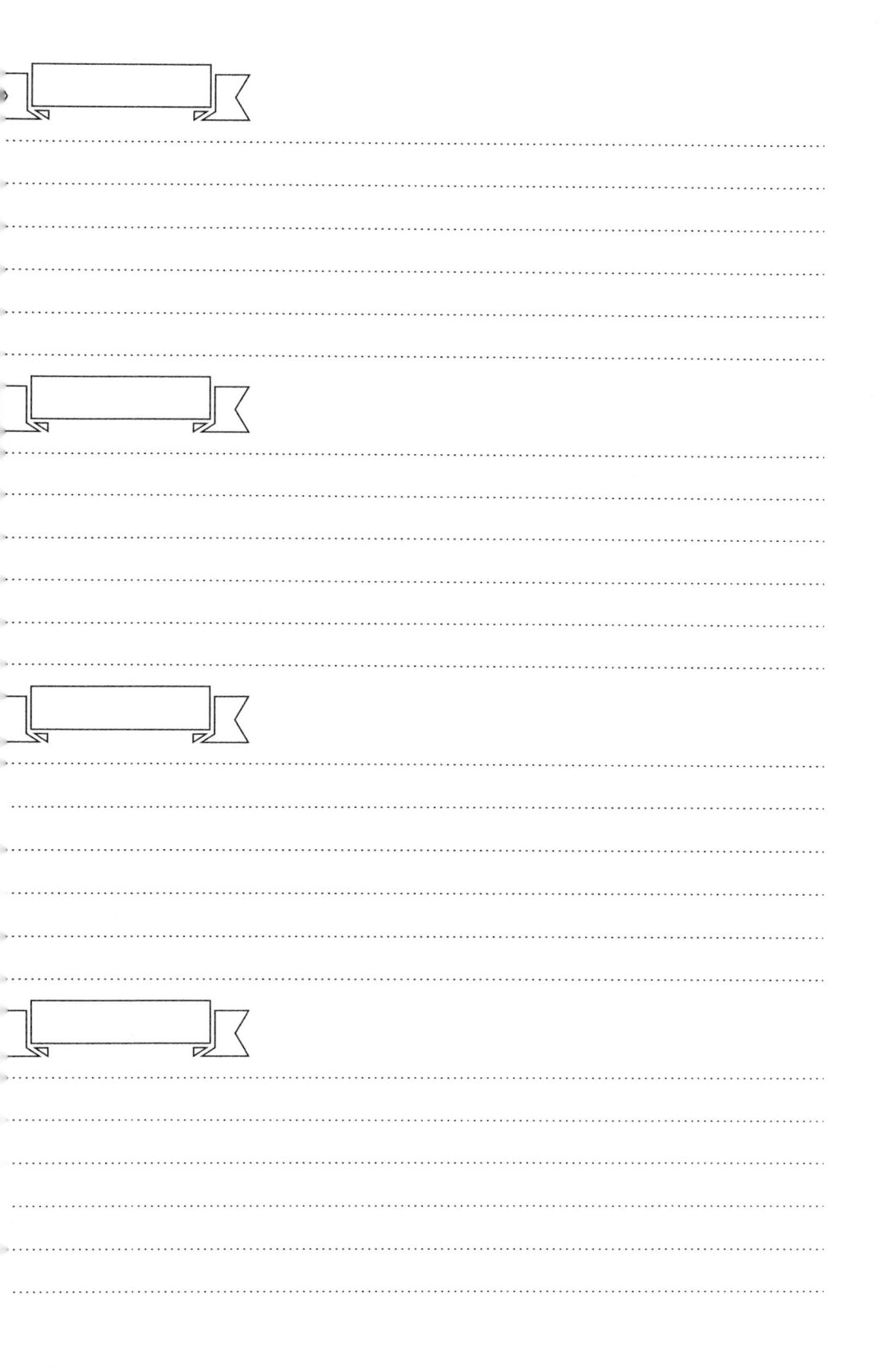

Printed in Great Britain
by Amazon